MATHS ACTIVITY BOOK 1

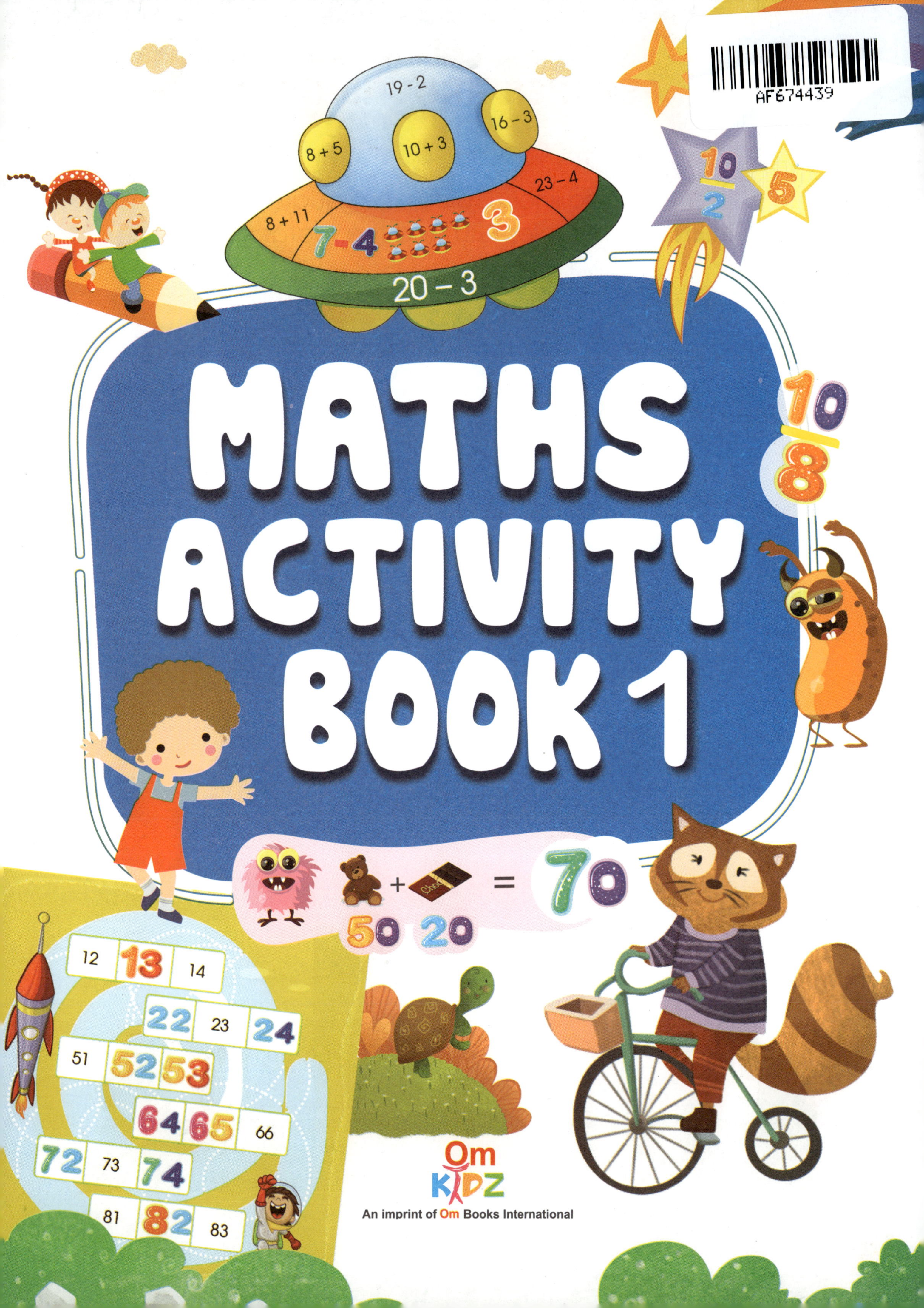

Om KIDZ
An imprint of Om Books International

SHAPES AROUND US

Trace over the dotted lines. Colour the squares **YELLOW**, the circles **GREEN**, the triangles **RED** and the rectangles **BLUE**.

ALMOST SHAPES

Look at the objects below. Their shapes are almost like the shapes you have learnt about. Can you match these objects to the correct shapes? One is done for you.

STAR HOP

Help Angus the Alien visit our planet by following the star path. Fill up the empty stars with the missing numbers.

ROCKET COUNT

Axl the Astronaut wants to get inside the rocket, but he must solve the puzzle first! Look at the numbers and fill in the ones that appear before, after or in between.

12		14

	23	

51		

		66

	73	

81		83

ACROSS THE UNIVERSE

This astronaut wants to go on a tour of the universe. Help him go from one planet to the other, but solve the sums on each planet first!

$$\begin{array}{r} 4 \\ +\ 5 \\ \hline \end{array}$$

$$\begin{array}{r} 10 \\ +\ 9 \\ \hline \end{array}$$

$$\begin{array}{r} 8 \\ +\ 9 \\ \hline \end{array}$$

$$\begin{array}{r} 2 \\ +\ 9 \\ \hline \end{array}$$

ASCENDING ALIENS

Help the aliens reach their spaceships by rearranging the numbers on their paths in an ascending order.

14		32		19	
10		41		8	
18		29		18	
21		35		4	
27		15		5	
5		23		6	

DESCENDING DEBRIS

Stop the flying debris from falling on our planet! Rearrange the numbers in descending order to save our planet.

22	11	44	33	55	66	88	99

15	18	14	19	10	13	7	23

59	42	67	63	82	94	51	35

SUBTRACTING SPACESHIPS

Solve the sums next to the aliens and cross out the correct number of spaceships. Write the answer in the box to help the aliens know how many spaceships they need.

10 – 8 =

5 – 4 =

9 – 2 =

7 – 4 =

12 – 6 =

4 – 0 =

8 – 3 =

6 – 2 =

SHAPE-SHIP

Trace over the shapes and colour the picture to complete the spaceship.

ASTROCODE

Solve the sums to crack the code and colour the spaceship.

Code: **RED** 17, **BLUE** 12, **YELLOW** 13, **GREEN** 19, **BLACK** 15.

SPACE QUIZ

Look at the pictures and answer the questions.

How many spaceships are travelling in space?

How many aliens are waiting to meet us?

How many stars do you see?

How many rockets are ready to take off?

ORDINAL PATH

Give these planets the correct ordinal numbers so the Space Kid knows how to visit them in the correct order. One is done for you.

ALIEN ADDITION

Help the alien solve the sums written on the comets.

39 + 17 =

25 + 10 =

21 + 9 =

31 + 20 =

32 + 5 =

42 + 7 =

FILLER FUN

Help Alexa the Astrogirl fill in the missing numbers to complete the sums.

18 + _____ = 24

24 + _____ = 32

17 + _____ = 23

10 + _____ = 30

9 + _____ = 19

29 + _____ = 33

41 + _____ = 52

39 + _____ = 43

CLOUD COUNTING

Subtract the sums in the clouds to clear the sky.

39 – 12 = ☐

42 – 10 = ☐

23 – 17 = ☐

48 – 32 = ☐

24 – 15 = ☐

17 – 15 = ☐

44 – 33 = ☐

WORDY WOES

Help the astronauts solve these word problems for the aliens.

I had 5 spaceships. My brother broke 2. How many were left with me?

My planet had 10 lakes. 4 of them dried up. How many do we have now?

I saw 8 meteorites on my way. 6 of them burst into flames. How many were left?

MULTIPLYING METEORITES

Solve the sums on the meteorites before they fall on our planet!

2 × 2 =

3 × 4 =

6 × 2 =

5 × 3 =

3 × 7 =

7 × 4 =

$2 \times 8 =$

$4 \times 8 =$

$9 \times 5 =$

$6 \times 6 =$

$7 \times 7 =$

$8 \times 9 =$

DIVIDE AND ROAM

Solve the sums on the stars below.

10 ÷ 2 =

18 ÷ 3 =

24 ÷ 4 =

20 ÷ 5 =

30 ÷ 6 =

49 ÷ 7 =

27 ÷ 3 =

36 ÷ 4 =

21 ÷ 7 =

2 ÷ 2 =

40 ÷ 5 =

12 ÷ 6 =

TIME TRAVELLER

Help the aliens tell the time by looking at the clocks below.

TIMELY MATCH

Match the clocks to the correct time on the spaceships.

WEEKLY WONDER

Fill up the rocket with the days of the week in their correct order. One is done for you.

MONTH MANIA

The aliens want to know about our planet. Help them out by filling the blanks with the correct month name.

Which is the first month of the year? ______________

Which is the fifth month of the year? ______________

In which month do you celebrate Christmas? ______________

In which month do you celebrate Children's Day? ______________

In which month do you celebrate India's Independence Day? ______________

SUPER SORTER

Help the Super Alien sort our months by numbering them in the correct order.

June

September

August

February

January

November

December

March

May

October

April

July

SHOPPING SPREE

These little aliens went shopping, but don't know anything about money. Can you add up the things they bought and tell them what they need to pay?

SPACE MAZE

Help the aliens find their way back home through the space maze. Follow the path with the correct number order.

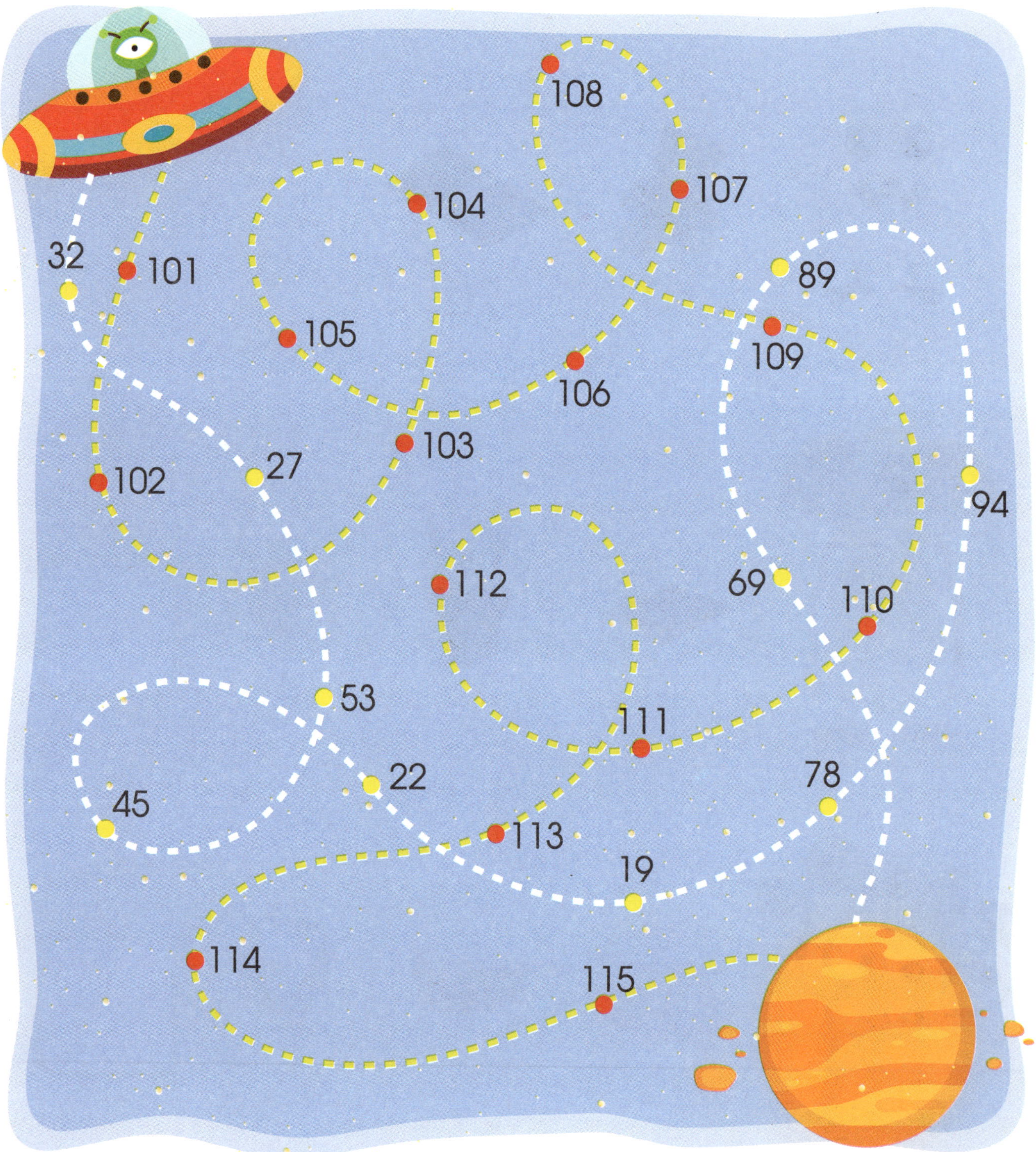

ANSWERS

Page 3

Page 4

Page 5

Page 6 Page7

Page 8

Q1. 14 10 18 21 27 5

Ans. 5 10 14 18 21 27

Q2. 32 41 29 35 15 23

Ans. 15 23 29 32 35 41

Q3. 19 8 18 4 5 6

Ans. 4 5 6 8 18 19

Page 9

Q1. 22 11 44 33 55 66 88 99

Ans. 99 88 66 55 44 33 22 11

Q2. 15 18 14 19 10 13 7 23

Ans. 23 19 18 15 14 13 10 7

Q3. 59 42 67 63 82 94 51 35

Ans. 94 82 67 63 59 51 42 35

Pages 10-11

10 – 8 = 2

5 – 4 = 1

9 – 2 = 7

7 – 4 = 3

12 – 6 = 6

4 – 0 = 4

8 – 3 = 5

6 – 2 = 4

Page 13

Page 14

Page 15

Page 16

39 + 17 = 56

25 + 10 = 35

21 + 9 = 30

31 + 20 = 51

32 + 5 = 37

42 + 7 = 49

ANSWERS

Page 17

18 + 6 = 24
24 + 8 = 32
17 + 6 = 23
10 + 20 = 30
9 + 10 = 19
29 + 4 = 33
41 + 11 = 52
39 + 4 = 43

Page 18

39 – 12 = 27
42 – 10 = 32
23 – 17 = 6
48 – 32 = 16
24 – 15 = 9
17 – 15 = 2
44 – 33 = 11

Page 19

Q1. I had 5 spaceships. My brother broke 2. How many were left with me?
Ans. 3
Q2. My planet had 10 lakes. 4 of them dried up. How many do we have now?
Ans. 6
Q3. I saw 8 meteorites on my way. 6 of them burst into flames. How many were left?
Ans. 2

Page 20 | Page 21 | Page 22 | Page 23

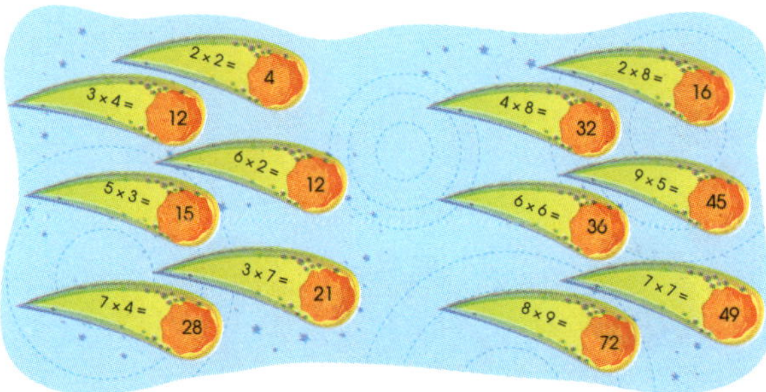

Page 24

Page 25

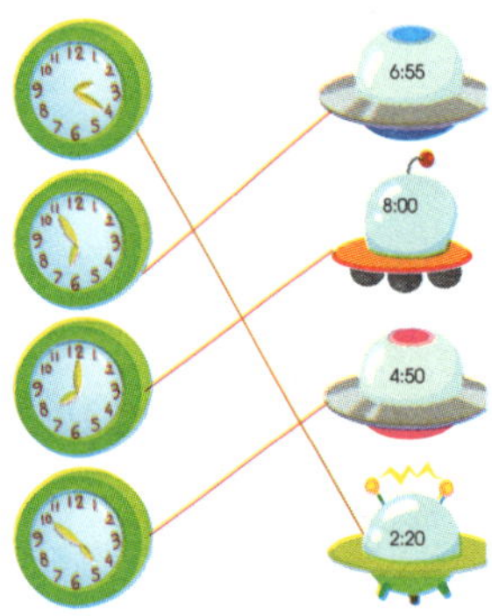

Page 26

Sunday	1
Monday	2
Tuesday	3
Wednesday	4
Thursday	5
Friday	6
Saturday	7

Page 27

Q1. Which is the first month of the year?
Ans. January
Q2. Which is the fifth month of the year?
Ans. May
Q3. In which month do you celebrate Christmas?
Ans. December
Q4. In which month do you celebrate Children's Day?
Ans. November
Q5. In which month do you celebrate India's Independence Day?
Ans. August

Page 28

Page 29

Q1. 1 teddy bear (50) + 1 chocolate (20) = 70

Q2. 1 book (40) + 1 plant (15) + 1 plate (14) = 69

Q3. 1 dress (25) + 1 sandwich (5) + 1 globe (32) = 62